Locomotive of Mangled Parts

poems by

G.R. Kramer

Finishing Line Press
Georgetown, Kentucky

Locomotive
of Mangled Parts

Copyright © 2023 by G.R. Kramer
ISBN 979-8-88838-222-6 First Edition
All rights reserved under International and Pan-American Copyright Conventions. No part of this book may be reproduced in any manner whatsoever without written permission from the publisher, except in the case of brief quotations embodied in critical articles and reviews.

ACKNOWLEDGMENTS

The following poems have appeared in the following journals or received the following distinctions:

"The Ancestors Take Questions About Your DNA Test Results" was a finalist for the 2023 Bedford Competition
"An Old Woman Reflects" was first published by *West Trade Review*
"Cavity" was first published by *Red Savina Review*
"The Cicadas Alone Will Mourn Us" was first published in *Global City Review*
"Eclipse" was first published as "Dark Orb" by *Harbinger Asylum*
"The Good Witch of the West Side" and "Three Thirty Nine" were first published in the *Oddville Press*
"Hamlet's Father" was a finalist for the Fourth Annual Sewanee Review Poetry Contest, and was first published in *Superpresent Magazine*
"Honeysuckle and Flaming Creeper" was a finalist for the *Arts & Letters* 2021 Annual Prize. That poem, together with "The Last Aspen Stand;" "Passover/Easter 2020;" "Mud Chameleon" as "Different Kinds of Mud;" and "The Hole in the Poem;" was first published in *Sixfold Magazine*
"Hospice Policy:" was first published by *Torrid Literary Journal*
"Let Us Take This" and "Locomotive" as "In the Beginning" were first published by *Map Literary*
"Roadkill" was a finalist in the *Winter Anthology* 2021 Annual Contest, and was first published in the *Winter Anthology*
"Schrödinger's Cat" was first published in *Thimble Magazine*
"Soldier" was first published in *Mudfish*

Special thanks to my wife Cathy for giving me the love, support, patience and space to write these. Thanks as well to the gifted poets of the tiny but mighty Bear & Wreck poetry workshop, Corbett Buckley, Mary Anna Dunn and Marti Stevens, for their helpful comments on several of these poems as they took shape.

Publisher: Leah Huete de Maines
Editor: Christen Kincaid
Cover Art: Photo (top) by Jacek Dylag on Unsplash; Photo (bottom) by Larry Costales on Unsplash
Author Photo: Catherine K. Kramer
Cover Design: Elizabeth Maines McCleavy

Order online: www.finishinglinepress.com
  also available on amazon.com

Author inquiries and mail orders:
Finishing Line Press
PO Box 1626
Georgetown, Kentucky 40324
USA

Table of Contents

LOCOMOTIVE	1
THE HOLE IN THE POEM	2
SCHRÖDINGER'S CAT	3
ROADKILL	4
HOSPICE POLICY:	5
THE CICADAS ALONE WILL MOURN US	6
HAMLET'S FATHER	8
MEMORY OF THE CHILD	9
LAST WALK IN DARK HILLS	10
PRAYER OF QUEEN GERTRUDE	11
THREE THIRTY NINE	12
MUD CHAMELEON	13
AN OLD WOMAN REFLECTS	14
PASSOVER/EASTER 2020	15
REGENESIS	16
CAVITY	17
ECLIPSE	19
THE LAST ASPEN STAND	20
TOM'S COVE	22
SOLDIER	24
UKRAINE HAIKU	25
THE ANCESTORS ARRIVE	27
THE ANCESTORS TAKE QUESTIONS ABOUT YOUR DNA TEST RESULTS	28
LET US TAKE THIS	29
HONEYSUCKLE AND FLAMING CREEPER	30
RUINS OF GEDI	31
COOKING, SEX, LIFE AND DEATH	32
THE GOOD WITCH OF THE WEST SIDE	33
PRETTY OK	35
LIFE IN A JAR	36

Locomotive
> "It is hard indeed to notice anything for which the languages available to us have no description." Alan Watts

In the beginning was heard
the brilliant word,
babbling of its birth.
Then the sentence clattered an entrance,
drunk metronome,
locomotive of mangled parts,
clacking on untrusty tracks,
snake straight
but shifted in their rusty bolts,
molting rolling thoughts.
It is the thing that gets lost
trying to explain itself.

This sentence,
conceived in the mind to die in meaning,
lumbering locution,
a listing headlamp and a whistle,
bridges darkness to darkness,
blind to much.
It leaves us still blind in the bright night.

Every sentence seems a failure born
on a dying tongue, yet sparking
up rails of light, a convolution
rolling to its distant point.
It does not see how the noun
decays in its womb or the verb
conjugates toward flowers,

riding this line to the next station.
There it may change to westbound
but never
                                        slip off the page,
skedaddling for a newspaper and coffee.
I remember a sentence like a hooded head,

lucent and lost,
lurching down the unlit path.

Where went the beveled edge
of the blade of language?
What is this word.
Why is this glory.

The Hole in the Poem

    It was termites, I think,
that bored   out the heart
of this   poem. Yet
the poem   still asks: why
is the hole   in the poem
        its heart? Less is more

     for a poem, but imagine
  if a magician's sleeve eclipsed the center of
the moon: a lacuna   cratering out the lunar
heart, a coreless   moon would now climb
the black   leaves of trees—
only a   peephole to
            Cygnus,
            Cat's Eye
           Nebula, Lyra
           and Vega C.

No memory,   no feeling, no minding
its leave, just our   sadness watching the heart
of the moon fall in the wordless sea. Less is less

for the moon. More or less.
Or let me put it like this:
When the hole fell
from this poem
I stuffed it lumpy
with words for grief and love
until, luminous
with lovely grief,
it sank in that sea
like a moonstone.
Pull it
up by the stuffing
and the hole returns.
In the center

waves the argentine flaglet
of something new.

Schrödinger's Cat

Critics, if I had them, would say
I should use fewer words
and say more.
Yes.

My greatest critic is my cat.
I don't have a cat.
But if I did she would approve
when I scratched her belly.

A poem is like Schrödinger's cat:
curled on paper
both dead and alive
until a reader decides which.

Erwin Schrödinger wrote a poem
about his cat. Like all poems,
it was a thought experiment,
meandering a bit like this,

but in the guise of a science paper
dealing with quantum superpositioning.
It was not received quite as he intended,
as with any successful poem.

He wrote in free verse
and chose not to show off,
resisting German rhymes
for "quantum superpositioning."

What he meant as an absurdity (a)
folds on itself into something
in some deep sense true ($isdst$),
leaving a remainder of one stanza line.

The formula reduces to $a^2=isdst$,
which might be the solution to all poetry.
The critics missed that trick
and should be criticized for that.

Roadkill

Under manic sun,
the deer's heat
leaks
on the berm.

Before terrible stars,
the berm leaks
day heat
into antlered trees.

Hospice Policy:

"No Jokes After 8 PM."
After I cracked wise
your laughter filled the room
with a chandelier
of graceful ice angels.
The tears came later,
finally and with zeal,
nuzzling your dying head.
How lovely when
the glacier within thaws
drip by dear drop,
leaving newly carved landscape
and us
only this day
to explore it all.

The Cicadas Alone Will Mourn Us
> *17-year cicadas, the longest-lived insects, rise once*
> *from underground, mate and die.*

we gather as one drove then die
cycle-stamped brood from dark larvae
earthen seeded pupae upswarm
mass in choral trees songs burn air
copulate ovules silence again

we gather in fervid paradise
born from the eternal earth womb
where life was a buried name of death
shrill yammering lust detonates
skin piles scattered as sated leaves

we gather within the rising
juddering tymbal brood racket
rise in forests and field edges
echo in stone and glass canyons
live our full day on tar rivers

our army of eyes gather as one
we watched you build hollow towers
sat by your crowded deadly thoughts
mourned your years of plodding and pain
the brief flash in which you dwelt

we gather to remember time
before your bone dust fell on the land
your cruel unsteady ascendence
as you lowered yourselves we fought
to arise apart from the same ground

we gather together to praise
the small greatness of your tiny clutch
your earthen dead playing cleft tines
of broken genius as the song
of our bliss fell unheard to you

we gather above your fallen truths
your doubts
dissolved to dirt and fed us

we gather to begin again
again we sing all that we know:

the time for all doing is now
we gather as one drove then die.

Hamlet's Father

Daily I think of my father:
shroud of broken threads—
venom-tainted veins—
scalpel blunted on
his double-woven heart.

I did not expect last night
he would speak of it:
his memory gullied out—
asking in the dark
that I seek its sediments—

stand with him
in ravine, forest—
me, his echo,
raving for us
to weary hills
against this slow ravelling.

Memory of the Child

As the old roan mare lopes
on pushing the confusion
of cows rounded by the collies
across the mud flats,

the boy thinks ahead
and because his taut gaze
is never adrift of the bovine
ocean bob of haunches

to lose his track of each
from each and because
he wonders how time's
slack lariat snaps tight

to cinch dewlap flesh
even as his hondo
knots the herd
to memory,

the horse stumbles
light, the day behind,
cattle gone to night pens
then slaughter, and below

the TV's blare
the frayed old man,
bathed in dim light
in the chair of his mind

scatterings, a worn
peace warming him
with thoughts that still
measure a mile's trail

of time, recalls pieces
of that child's lost face,
the calm forms of beasts
returned to stable,

and how finally
none of it was wasted.

Last Walk in Dark Hills

In the swim of shivered fog that drapes a silver lunar breast
as I trace the entire world in the windless corvine forest
and trudge my way through the constant wake of life's icy crises
that purl slow around the path and frosted cumulous contours

lit by the covered moon so that clouds shade over imagined
clouds as Capricorn and Mars pin up a piece of sky—footfalls
of my steps stub and stumble over half-hidden thoughts, pull
silences from me amid the leaves long fallen thickly round

though many years' dried lines of rich spoor bury in splendid rot
and sum the total of some waning life: the doubtful trail blaze
and dark moon's hazy undoings drag me into a tidal
undertow (I feel the waves I feel the baffled wash of love

I dream I heal)—I hurry back to the hidden track that leads
toward enough—I run before myself like a scouting dog
(my face within now wind-whipped with faces of all forgotten)—
and look, is it time to give over, bone of gray moon out now?

Prayer of Queen Gertrude
    An imagined missing soliloquy from Act III of Hamlet

I crave return to the earth.
I who bore that boy
now must abide his destruction.

Whose image is it in this dark mirror
shadowed, candle lit, framed by white roses?
A lone woman, but not one waiting
for a sign from above,
from You,
the One who makes no signs.

For You I have no explanations,
nor for my husband, nor for my son,
though You and I both see him
in the doorway.

I think we see him the same way,
his mind wobbling, his dagger golden red
looking for a place to plunge,
as I hear a storm rising out of the garden, spreading
to my bedchamber. Like a heavy oak with clumsy limbs,
a fool falls from behind a curtain, run through by fear.

The end would now be so different
if either one of us cared more about it.
I am a mother, but not like You are a Father.
The world is Your body, but for all the world's noise
I have found You mute.
My body has been my voice, You have seen to that,
and my voice falls silent by my choice.

I have shame. You,
the Playwright of all this,
You have just Your contempt
for all of us, giving us only loss
to show Your power.

You will never be the light I call out to,
but only the blackness beyond.
I dismiss you,
as I will be dismissed.

Three Thirty Nine

according to the somnolent clock,
a pale green sun over her sleeping form

that I watch on her inward flight
through whichever cityscapes and jungles

her flicking eyelids choose.
I ebb in somnia and

dream that my dreams and hers
intertwine, waves washing down alleyways and

receding, oceans tugging
our difficult shorelines, each whitecap

a marriage of air and water,
a serrated roof over such depths

of lost wrecks, of water swinging
over the aloneness of green and black

krill as whale flukes crack
silver into the night air, swallowing stars

that perched above as she passed through
churches and pastures of her tangled country.

Each night our skin somnambulates
to places our bones cannot follow.
I stay up waiting.

Mud Chameleon

More mud than man,
I was made from spit
and dirt, descended
from a bog

now dried and cracked.
When the rain departed
I shone for an hour
under a high sun.

My minds remain many
heaps of fallen rose petals
in different shades of brown.
My one heart, disguised
coal black,
still pumps mud-thick blood
that squeaks—as if to ask.

The swamp grass rooted in me
before she came to set her toes,
and sink and stir such chemistries.
Out of dry grass and pebbles
we shape this together

and in the morning lie
with creation. Again the hawk
drifts overhead
and passes.
The child is now strong
but pain always steals again
for the wild God above.

Now I've become old mud,
these boots caked like blood
until mud and boots are one.
I wash my shadow in mud.
Has time changed you mud?
Do you still squeal your young question?

An Old Woman Reflects

The empty street sings
a cold song under
a silent spring sky
that coils my soul
in the same pale sadness
that I felt after
my husband's death.
Grape hyacinth and narcissus
call to my eyes
with colors that racket in my head.
Yet a part of me is numb.
No poem has ever witnessed more
than what I see
out the kitchen window.
Yet some part of me is numb.
My son sent me a video
of Italians serenading
their neighbors
in locked-down cities.
From apartment balconies
music draped
the streets in garlands.
Later I dreamt
of a ringing Milanese street
where I reached
to touch boughs
of dry flowers.
Wrapped in the oleanders
and asters I wished
to set my soul aflame
and sleep in its ashes.

Passover/Easter 2020

Since Eden never such a sanguine night.
After the slaughter in Goshen of all the flocks,
their cries abate in the last limb of light.
Against slave hut doors a blood tide knocks.
Moses chafes for the risen sun god's eye
then the furious flight to silent Sinai.

Contagions and devils stalk this spring
as willets and warblers ring and rage
over this and that malicious king,
over these just deserts, that minor plague,
over those years of Egypt grown dull and fat
and the hungers haunting Judea after that.

Another prophet offers up feeble explanations
for each lost child and blood-let lamb.
Fear lumbers today through divided nations
and down the snaking streets of tired Jerusalem
stumbles the risen son, a savior, an enemy
falling from this weedy Garden of Gethsemane.

Regenesis

> "The mind is its own place, and in itself
> Can make a heav'n of hell, a hell of heav'n."
> —John Milton, Paradise Lost.

Slashes of light
and thunder flood the world. The senseless see
how nothing drains from verdant hell, & smell
the stink of angels trapped in sewage rot.

For seven years and seven days
a sightless odd man struggled
with the mud of Eve & Adam,
with their choice to not be gods
but our parents,
as the buried golden ribs
of golems busted out of our softest dreams,
to a place in our minds big enough
to hold both heaven

& hell. Yes, we now admit
all our future wrongs,
how we too will blindly forge
a false confession, try again
the serpent's cage. Yes,

we will forever wander
from a first dark fire
to the last galactic black hole.

Even his condemned friend Galileo,
torn from Tuscany into the poem,
could not explain who allowed the asp
to escape the vivarium
or with what intention. Still

the Father fervidly dreams
his venomed angels
will make it right, pull wide

mortal wounds, climb inside
the one true cadaver
till the temple shakes out silver
& from the Calvary dusk
a hollow mouth wild awe open
cracks air with jagged praise.

Cavity

Your blind dentist,
cruel, kind one true dentist,
will see you at ten o'clock.
Let her fingers feel the deep recesses,
sorting good from rot,
let her gracey curette
pick inside the lip
of your angry gingiva.
Let her help you find where you begin
and where you end.
When the shadow of pain falls across,
let a mask seal in your breathing thoughts,
the thin nitrous oxide barrier all
that divides what is and what is not.
The x rays will miss them,
but let your blind dentist see
all the forgotten truths about you.

Let your dentist not be dead.
Let her live inside, playing you
in her imagination,
as you imagine her hands
playing over her ivory work.
If you do not know if she lives in you,
just know that she knows nothing
unknown also to you,
but she overwhelms your nothingness,
light mixing in darkness
and darkness in light. Later

let her billing office go unpaid.
The dunning letter will sit before you,
its cancelled forever stamps
and outstanding deductible clamoring
for the cunning emptiness of your cavity.

Every moment is a mystery,
a tangle of then, now and when,
according to her invisible diploma
above the porcelain spittoon,
silently watching over you,

forever agape and helpless,
mourning your extinct cavity,
amen.

Eclipse

What is the shadow of the restless Earth
if not a whisper to the deaf moon,
speaking of urges
and erasures over eons
on continental canvasses, half-forgotten
memories of volcanic torments
that could tease syzygy to lunacy?

Sunlight illumined off
the beaten lunar face
silhouettes an infant palimpsest,
nursed on obliviating
rain and wind, swaddled
in tectonic blankets.
A warm-hearted amnesiac,
innocent enabler,
the artful Earth shines over

airless ageless craters and pocks.
The tired Moon, worn by abuse,
counts up every tedious meteor blow.
Dead, cold and without too much hate
for the earth, that sibling
with one agate blue brown eye
has its selfish unrequited love,
has that too intimate orbital embrace.
After receiving a billion spring tides,
gifting a few Apollo footprints.
the moodless Moon is forever
the Earth's mark.

The Earth turns over fresh soil,
each new day begetting extinction
and birth of a new sun.
Every moment
a new river runs into a new sea.

Scales flash in water.
On coastal cliffs
what tiny shadows
exalt
the sister Moon?

The Last Aspen Stand

> *Aspen share a common root system, resulting in stands that are genetically a single tree. One such aspen stand in Utah is 80,000 years old—the largest and oldest living organism.*

The best of us
is at the root,
away from light,
probing for good
in dark. We are
a single tree, divided
above and below,
every part devotion
to a whole.

In each breath
live a hundred generations
of mastadons,
elk and nuthatch.
Out of what heart wood
do we worship the wind
with leaves like shimmering hands?
How many winters
have strengthened our fiber?
How many fires do we bear,
or saplings strangle in our shadow?

We feel our killers' footsteps
fall among us,
and we weep:
for our alikeness;
our mutual need;
our sense of selves;
our awe
of the other's strangeness;

your weak grasp on what you saw;
your blind visions and divisions
both within and without.
Even

as we die, you forget
that the core of all of us

is a heart woven of two fibers:

- one to heal,
- and one to harm.

Tom's Cove

Edge lines of water, grass
and sun-singed blue sky
fret their colors, cast nets
past shore birds afloat
in tidal shallows
to the rim of the world.

A fleet of gulls, terns,
ibis and herons
lie anchored and alert,
like their river of forebears
that stood watch
on ten million such radiant days,
ten million more when raindrops
pocked clear gray water.

Such assortments—
the arch of the egret's neck,
and the bleak oyster catcher
on its reef of shells.
Overhead ospreys crisscross
the bay patrolling
for fish. Flexing wet wings,
skinny chest thrust out,
a cormorant sits atop a buoy.

I tell Cathy that I try to learn not to think much
about the ways we gaze
at the salt marsh flats
though I know
that I could look more deeply.
One of life's funny conundrums, I start to say,
then there is a shift

and the osprey veer away.
The motley fleet sets sail, flapping
above the water to new respite,
a flock of nervous terns,
the ungainly lope
of a single great blue heron.
We look for the disturbance.

There it is,
high aloft,
a thick black line,
and white dot against the blue.
American bald eagle,
delicate patch
of menace, majestic
dot in the day,
circles awhile then drifts away.
The osprey return.
As things go on

I almost see how
the laughing gulls' cries
and wheeling ospreys
are to us as we are
to the cattails and salt hay,
as is the marsh grass
to the blue ebb of water and sky.

Soldier

Sometimes a soldier
will start laughing
in the middle of the battle,
at nothing and for no reason.

It is as though he is somewhere else,
helmet strapped on
at his old school desk,
where someone carved his name

with a bayonet.
His laughter ends,
and he thinks of his lover,
the times he was sorry,

the silence of God,
the bomb's orange petals
opening,
and a joke he has yet to tell.

Ukraine Haiku

all across the road
blood of butchered   root in cracks
seed of black spring   bloom

weapon

below white flowers
we lie with the fray of bees
nowhere people are

loud

mir meant peace to both
when trees leafed over laughter
now   stumps   stand   their   ground

silent

Their portrait   stained   red
parlor tatters   open sky
empty sniper eyes

annihilate

dear   scor   ched   children
let's play in the   gutted   car
front seat   parents sleep

witness

may the good endure
tanks missiles sunflowers plows
may the lost   return

explosive

see how the flies help
keep down   the odor of rot
old men in ditches

artillery

war machines rust out
wind blown blood loam covers steppe
lily bulbs open

memory

nations' lies take life
empires feed   death to the dead
human history

for   got   ten

mothers of soldiers
whose blood drains to the black sea
mothers of soldiers

The Ancestors Arrive
"Why consult the dead on behalf of the living?" Isaiah 8:19.

From faded sepia prints, down.
From gods of Mount Olympus, down.
From unspeakable saints, down.
From innocent sinners, down.
From pebbles on tombstones, down.

From ovens, yeast, yarn and stitchery,
from Masai hunting on the Serengeti,
from covens of red Magyar witchery,
from forgotten mothers suckled by their babes,
from unknown fathers fled after rapes,
from old lies your grandparents concocted,
from new truths DNA testing unlocked,
from an odd mole on my ass or your thigh,
from the sky, from the ground
down.

They only descend into this lost world
because a blood line calls them
from the hollows of our raving hearts
to rescue us, repulsive as we seem,
in our smooth bodies and tempered minds.
We have no family besides this to teach us

how we will abide, if we ever did,
in those darknesses divided
by the light flash of life.
The ancestors are not just dead.
Our faces are etched
to their funeral masks.
So set heel to shovel,
burn incense and scatter
ashes, leave fresh lavender
on their graves.
Why consult the dead
on behalf of the living?
Make altars out of this life.

The Ancestors Take Questions About Your DNA Test Results

Carry it from our shadow cave,
wrap it in thick quilts of fiction
stitched by the thin luminous threads
of molecules. This dull query
mirrors your life of mountainous
suspicions. What coin are you owed—

you who imagine the dismal days
of the dead are spent mining
radioactive half-lies? Child,
we don't care if our story reads straight,
we have nothing to spend but time
but not time enough to please you.

Your inheritance is a shamble
of science, star waste and love
fused inside chemical spirals,
amoebas mutated to bastards,
blood transfigured from venom,
slave traders costumed as saints.

The geology of life compacts
into strata of lost worlds, squeezes
petty hearts to dust, degenerates
to weary atoms, then repairs
to gold. Like conscious continents,
we break what is broken in us.

As chromosomes grind together,
as the volcanic joins to the glacial,
as the living are tied to the dead,
as a human finds a human in crowds,
an unlikely trace lights the dust,
this decayed radiance of love.

Let Us Take This
    In memory of Allan Wiley.

Let us take this.
If not the tendrils of the garden vine.
If not this park's great oak tree
reaching out from the deep earth.
If not our rambles roped like planets
into ellipses of that leafy sun.
Or the moon winching
up the coarse twine of oak limbs,
a spidery lattice under ivory lunar light.

Let us take this.
If not the tippling wind plucking the woods.
If not the rustling laundry of winter leaves.
If not the sole blue balloon
lofting unbound on your children's laughter,
Or the liquid guitar chords that you loved
trickling through magnetic pickups,
dreaming us gods pretending we are not.

Let us take more than the slack casings of regret:
that your light cut just a bit into the disenchanting dusk,
that the trail washes out at water's edge,
that you left your name on bottles of bitter pills
churning in the swell of your nightstand's tides.

Let us take knowing that others may be cured
of the comfort of hiding inside the longing to be known.
Let them take what they need to rebuild
their battered lighthouse
where the doubtful think that only they can clearly see.
Let us take grief as a planting, a seed of faith,
even if we only spin like mayflies
round a light we saw go out.

Then take with you the things not left behind.
Strap them to the great heart
that you carry lightly from this world.
We are stronger
laden with absent weight.

Honeysuckle and Flaming Creeper
On reading Terrance Hayes

As you said, there never was a black male hysteria.
It is a wonder to ponder the spent lifetimes
Stacked under a lineage of kingly goons
In Money Mississippi. Or lying scattered
Like bone bits in other not much better places
And still not mirror the madness in the faces.
Imagine instead planting your good feet in dirt
And letting the sprouts spread out for miles.
Many may be pulled up, or frisked down,
But still they tendril, lancing hearts,
Doubling back on themselves, entwining,
Alive but speaking for the weary dead.
You should see them, all these strong green ropes,
Wrapping a restless house in fiery hopes.

Ruins of Gedi

Gedi was an ancient Arab trading town on the Kenyan coast of the Indian Ocean. Settled sometime after 1000 CE, it was suddenly abandoned in the 1600s. The fate of its inhabitants is unknown.

Clear finger moon strums
on ancient stone walls
on the hills above a muffled ocean.
The town within lies empty.
No blood, no bullets, no mass graves.
Pottery and fineries left behind.
Gates unlatched, responsibilities fled.
Fear and sorrow lie muzzled
between the town walls
and the thick forest.

Perhaps only the women,
still and silent, stayed.
Stemmed the despair
that spooled in the night,
unflinching, steadfast. Stanched
the miasma.
Later they called out.
No answer came from the wave-
beaten shoreline
or the enfolding jungle.

By dawn the women had become
ghosts, mourning the unbroken
bread loaves, the cold ashes
of kitchen fires, the impressed shapes
that still filled beds,
the silence of remembered songs.
The men and children
had taken a silver trail out to sea
where none could hear the other's voice.

Cooking, Sex, Life and Death

The machinery of internet pornography
is a blender of whirling blades
gelding the grip, grind
and grunt of it.
Courtship was once,
maybe, a coupling
of growth and hunger,
a chiffon flowering in a garden
in the first fecund dawn,
but the modern mind has moved on

out to the country
where the factory farms
devote a few capons and fryers
for copulation quota,
while the pullets cluck in hutches
over clutches of barren eggs.
In town, lust now piles
in grocery aisles,
until rung up

and later cracked and whipped
like eggs on a hot pan
in the kitchen.
Then upstairs
on the creaking pallet
the fry cook lays
with the butcher,
their clefts and cracks
mending in a moment
of simple human need.
Basted in cooling sweat,
a fertile red joy
floats just beyond
joined bodies
waiting for its birth,
poaching inside
God's fevered ovarium.

The Good Witch of the West Side

Into the rattling subway silence
came her familiar moonlit pitch,
                her worn smile always   on like an
occult crown,
her thoughts radiated   outward, saturated
inward
                the crevices of her mind.
The songs that rang out from her,
                                      nonsensical and
deeply true, echoed
      off the walls of headlines   to be long remembered by some,
                      like certain moments
with small children. When she ended her chirping and
hopped away to the next car,
            she left unspoken   words,
caught like flies
in flypaper, in a swaying breeze
                              of silent straphanging
passengers. Some days

she reached
into her rumpled bag for
the clay bowl   from her lost daughter.

She told a gray man in a gray hat   on the Number 3 train
how she swept the cars with her invisible broom,
he asked if that meant she was
the Good Witch of the West Side,
and they laughed together.
She saw him often on the train after that   and traded smiles.

Once she showed him the holy letters
from her children,
telling of their lives in foster care.
She wanted to fly to them   but her wings were trapped

In glue.
Instead
she asked him

if he could,
he said
he was sorry
but,
her glance wandered
from his face
like a ghost of a bird
and somehow
                                            she flew to the next car
                                                                                      on
stumps of broken wings.

He never saw her again after that.
Mornings later he was dozing in his seat.
He opened his eyes at his stop.
Next to him he found
                                            a small bowl of dead flies.

Pretty OK

Like an old pop song,
It isn't too cruel or kind.
Instead of ice cream
it is low-fat sorbet.
It lacks moxie,
just a feeble label
for the average human
on the average day. Sneer
if you must at its seeming mediocrity,
like serving Socrates
moldy hemlock
in a plastic cup.
We could think it a caustic
itty bromide
for just showing up. But.
If all the sublime
was squeezed
out of the fruitful world
and the terrible
too, till it was a tidy vapid
bitty tangerine, ponder
then how rapidly
we would tear
it asunder,
leave it ten-eighteenths rotten—
like our hearts,
misbegotten.

                    theworld
            waslarge,thentimewashed,
    shrunk   small
                Life in a Jar
    inside   and
    out.alligotwasthislousyteeshirt,
    butirememberdimensions,wind
    owlight,feeling,sotherescontent
                mentintheend.

www.ingramcontent.com/pod-product-compliance
Lightning Source LLC
Chambersburg PA
CBHW022123090426
42743CB00008B/978

9798883822226